OPERA DI CERA

# Opera di Cera

## Kelley Swain

*Valley Press*

First published in 2014 by Valley Press
Woodend, The Crescent, Scarborough, YO11 2PW
www.valleypressuk.com

ISBN: 978-1-908853-36-3
Cat. no. VP0055

A CIP record for this book is
available from the British Library

Printed and bound in Great Britain by
TJ International Ltd, Padstow, Cornwall

www.valleypressuk.com/authors/kelleyswain

# Contents

## Acknowledgements

My heartfelt thanks are due to Madame Verity Chianea, whose home in Les Adrets de L'Esterel in winter 2011 provided the ideal space in which to write the *Opera*, to Dr Anna Maerker of King's College London, whose writings on La Specola provided a thorough grounding in the history of the anatomical waxworks, to Tanya Marcuse, whose photographs of the waxworks provided inspiration and the ideal book cover, to Richard Barnett, Simon Barraclough, Lorraine Mariner, and Sarah Westcott, for thorough edits and discussion on various drafts, to Richard Barnett also for suggesting the title, to Jamie McGarry of Valley Press, for his enthusiasm and skill in the profession of publishing, and to my friends and family, for listening to me talk about obscure findings in the history of anatomical museums, and for encouraging me always.

*for Richard Barnett*

*'In nova fert animus mutatas dicere formas
corpora'*

Ovid, *Metamorphoses*

*'My soul is wrought to sing of forms transformed
to bodies new and strange!'*

Translation: Brookes Moore

*Florence, 1775:*

The Royal Museum of Physics and Natural History opens to the public, soon receiving international acclaim.

It is home to a collection of human anatomical models made of wax, the most famous of which is the female 'anatomical Venus', a recumbent life-sized figure with real human hair, whose torso disassembles to reveal a foetus in the womb.

The Museum gains the nickname 'La Specola' because it houses an astronomical observatory, but 'this colloquial title also captured what was expected of the visitor: "to speculate, contemplate, view, or observe a thing attentively". [Anna Maerker.]

*Setting:*

Florence, 1774.

## Characters

| | |
|---|---|
| VENUS | Narrator/Anatomical Model |
| TERESA ('TESS') | Artists' Model |
| GIANCINTO GUIDETTI ('CINTIO') | Museum Assistant |
| CLEMENTE SUSINI | Chief Wax Modeller |
| MASTER FELICE FONTANA | Director of Museo La Specola |

*Prologue*

## VENUS

Wide granite stairs, high-windowed halls, and finally, the tower;
clicking clocks on seven floors that tightly mark the hours.

A Tuscan-yellow castle, more like a citadel,
follows Creation from the womb to heaven or to hell.

Still and airless silent rooms with hundred staring eyes –
tigers, zebras, bats, baboons, all silenced in their hides.

The octagonal tower blinks a monocle to the night,
while window after window shutters out Italian light.

Wax, feather, fur and skin remain suspended in the dusk,
while life in Florence tumbles on with bustle and with busk.

The men within La Specola are watching, and they watch,
for their demanding work requires caution, calls reproach.

Here I have a tale to tell of how the wax was made,
the famous Venus, who even now, is apex of her trade.

Prepare your heart, stomach, and mind, before we can begin
the story of the tragic Florentine Pygmalion.

*Act One*

## TERESA

Each hair must be golden, or plucked.
Each pore must be purged, smoothed.

Teeth scrubbed, whitened, gleaming
with powder of arsenic. Skin gilded
with powder of saffron. Feet buffed.

'Her skin is like porcelain, her skin
is like gold.'
                    This depends on light.

'Observe her swanlike neck, the curve
at her breast.'
                    This depends on posture.

'Note her arching feet, her symmetrical
toes.'
                    This depends on balance.

They do not feel the sweat
in the crook of my underarm.

They do not hear the purr in my belly
as lunchtime nears, and passes.

They do not know the fears
that once monthly I will burst,

a crimson flood,

and be banished at the horror
that I am not of marble made.

## CINTIO

'*Baronfottuto!*' the cloaked man curses,
congealing from tomb-shadow to living flesh.

I drop my wicker basket. A hand
rolls out, reaches back in grey accusation,

followed by a tumble of soft shapes:
kidney, two lungs, tangle of intestine.

'I knew it – wastrel!' the cloaked man cries.
'Your Master Fontana shall pay – specimens

belong with the surgeons. Students need
these bodies; your Museum should not compete.'

I retreat; the man stalks into dark.

As if at prayer, I kneel at the familiar pit with a sigh.
In go the lungs. Then the hand, intestine, kidney.

The stillborn I pull from the wicker basket,
from the Hospital of the Innocents, should be tucked
into hallowed ground with all the lost orphans.
It, too, slaps into the pit.
Assistants have no time for pity.

I make my way twice each day to the Orphanage
for children, part or whole,
twice to Hospital Santa Maria Nuova,
for corpses full-grown.

I barely have time to eat.

Hunger rasps my stomach, while the ruined
side of my face twitches, stunned and twisted.

In the Royal Kitchens, before I was melted
and sent to work for the wax-makers,
I was warm and fed. Now I starve
while I handle the dead.

## SUSINI

Vesalius, Albinus, Haller, Vicq d'Azyr,
Loder, Soemmering, Weitbrecht, Hunter.

We prop up the tomes
with brushes, boxes, bones,
break their spines,
splatter them with turpentine.

Vesalius, Albinus, Haller, Vicq d'Azyr,
Loder, Soemmering, Weitbrecht, Hunter.

A corpse dissected for each image made,
(no, probably more,) exactly displayed.
The image is chosen, the dead compromised,
for thousands of waxes. For life, stylized.

Vesalius, Albinus, Haller, Vicq d'Azyr,
Loder, Soemmering, Weitbrecht, Hunter.

The Museum's goal, with each model cast:
creating waxworks to teach, to last.
I pray that once this work has ceased,
corpses stay buried. The dead, rest in peace.

## FONTANA

The space I rule lies in between
my Servant and my Sovereign:
Cintio and the Duke.

Enlightenment learnt through the eyes:
a perfect model, no surprise,
is understanding, proof.

Laws of Nature thus observed
the Grand Duke has the final word:
a Natural Right to rule.

La Specola is my Domain,
creating 'Model Citizens'
– I am nobody's fool.

Phase the First:

A dissector, highly skilled, prepares the base.
Fontana, often, or another, in his long-cast
shadow. Glossy organs
grease the table, impressions
of mortality; human remains detailed.

Phase the Second:

Plaster captures, inversely, detail
painstakingly revealed: a matrix, an impression
kept for years to make copies of organs;
flesh greased or waxed to smooth breach from cast,
a thread lain, umbilically, between plaster and base.

Phase the Third:

Final object, livelier than that on which it is based,
seems real, so lyric as to cast
doubt: does it live? Do the organs
move? A lung may give the uncanny impression
of breath; an eye wink, a heart beat. Details.

## CINTIO

I've worked my fingers down each grimy crack:
this city's byways and wine-cool basements.
With surgeons, students I'm bound to cross paths,
each man seeking illegal replacements.

Two hundred corpses complete a whole wax.
My dark magic is one of effacement,
I know well. Each errand secretly wrapped
so my Master is safe from abasement.

Heavy-cloaked, I knock. Within, a weak scream,
lamenting failed birth; ragged labour.
Moist walls groan with distress; faint candles weep.

I offer to remove the source of grief.
Poor wretch. Copper coins: I am her saviour.
My baskets, gravid. The Master is pleased.

SUSINI

The candle, burning low, reveals her shape,
dark valley between buttocks; curve of spine.
She turns with skill, arranges, lays supine
—I carve the shadow at her long neck's nape.

Here I sit, as sculptor. She, the Grace.
My eyes and hands must measure out her form.
Her skin: the finest cloak she's ever worn.

I silently send up a wish to Fate.

Perfection stretches, taut, upon her loom.
Her perfume weaves a thickly-spiced incense.

'Fore autumn turns the thimble of the moon,
Fate, show her love for me – I won't presume –
no, *prove* her love for me, as recompense
for my hard work. I want no other boon.

## FONTANA

I find it soothes my mind to have a treat.
Disturbed by salivation, I gasp, waking:
go to buy the butcher's finest meat.

Dissection's rich rewards cannot be sweet –
in my fine work, no flesh am I forsaking,
but find it soothes my mind to have a treat.

Flies converge in city's grasping heat,
and specimens grow too ripe for the taking.
I go to buy the butcher's finest meat –

ensure my rising debts remain discreet.
Suspect he thinks things sacrosanct I'm breaking,
but find it soothes my mind to have a treat.

On the table lies a tongue from down the street.
The bodies, they embody all my nerves and shaking.
To soothe, I buy the butcher's finest meat.

Assuaged of all my hungers, I can sleep.
Salivation my salvation in the making:
I find it soothes my mind to have a treat
and go to buy the butcher's finest meat.

TERESA

Nude, not bare.
Each sense is quickened, cloaked in stimuli:
warm sunlight in afternoon, pungent linseed fumes,
the whisper of a rinsed brush, the kiss of bristles to canvas,
the mingling of oils upon wooden palettes.

When one paints my arm, birthmark, a breast, I know.
I feel the weight of his mind on it. I offer this material,
feel their eyes on my figure, stand in for saint or goddess.

Then: a shattering of all expectation.
Susini looks.
The young artist: handsome, polite, gracious,
the one I admire from afar.
Susini sees.

And how can I conceal the flush pricking each follicle of skin?
I am used to being seen, to standing full unclothed,
yet now, beneath Susini's gaze, I am exposed.
Hide the erection of nipple! Suppress my blushing cheek!
Hold on to the cavernous falling – but no, I cannot move or speak.
I fear lest anyone see. Will they guess? I cannot meet their eyes.
They mix, they brush, they rinse, they level and foreshorten:
examine me minutely, yet none express surprise.

None note the change that trembles in my knees.
No one but Susini sees.

CINTIO

Expectant mothers sometimes fail.
She has a shock; her face turns pale,
the child she is carrying
turns rotten; becomes threatening.
If it is born, but doesn't wail,
if Hope and Fate dance on the scales –
we'll never know the turns entailed,
if life is lost through tarrying;
the woe; the woe.

At worst, she'll have a haemorrhage,
and neither mum nor babe may live.
An errant womb's certain rejection,
or God imparting a correction
on a union he won't forgive:
the woe; the woe.

The pork fat, fennel, in my cellar,
packed and pricked and wrapped with twine,
cures beneath the place I dwell, where
the pork fat, fennel, in my cellar,
hangs until I sit to dine.
*Finocchiona* tastes divine –
that pork fat, fennel, in my cellar
stuffed and stabbed and wrapped with twine.

TERESA

Will his hands be rough or smooth,
will his scent be turpentine,
may I choose?

Will his scent be orange boughs,
my limbs encouraging as vines,
my lips bruised?

Will his hands entwine my hair,
pull, revealing milk-throat, bare,
and, lips to mine,

drink me to a quavering line,
into his muse?

SUSINI

She is an addiction I do not wish to quit
            – I have barely tasted her effects.

She is Prosecco riddling my mind.
Laudanum flooding my nerves.

She gets my blood up.

                    I am going deliciously mad.

FONTANA

The limbs, and skins, in my Museum
trussed and tweezed and teased aside
mock the art that happens there.
The limbs, and skins, in my Museum
will all their rags incarnadine.
God's craft I'm sure to show divine.
Those limbs, those skins, in my Museum,
transformed to wax: fame will be mine.

*Act Two*

TERESA

Your fingers strum, scrape:
my lemon pith is sweet, you say,
and you grow younger: lustrous,
each time richer. I grow addicted.
Until I am raw, hollow, scooped out,
polished, an offering, this chalice
pelvic girdle: fountain of life, youth,
the grail you tongue, swallow.
But you are salt-thick
and I grow parched on you,
skin and sweat, longing.
A delirious feast: I could live for days
on the scent of you alone.

You send the slick home, drug
my senses, perfume my nose
my eyes weep your fluids
which I have consumed,
but my every bite and suck
yields more of me to you
until I am entirely folded in,
vine-wrapped by flesh and limb,
your coarse hair at groin, armpit,
chin a dense carpet; my musky one,
my blood-thick love.

Just below the point of my navel,
my guts hunger and cry for you:
feed me your flavours. Drown
me, let us mingle, infuse me
with your vital essence.

## SUSINI

I will sweat over your pancreas.
My hands will shake whilst I shape your kidneys.
I must perfect the redness of your aorta;
how shall I capture the gold of your skin?

You are far from me now though I plunge
into your bronchial cavities, furrow my brow
over your pelvic girdle. I am your god, shaping
rib, rib and rib, but you come before, you,
my Venus, my living, breathing goddess.

Now, gentlemen: a vivisection.
Leave if you cannot bear it.

See this stray bitch, tied down?
Her stretched belly made Master Fontana's decision.
She will slide open like a grapefruit, pink and glistening.
You shall learn much from this.

Palette: sponges, chisels, winking knives.
Canvas: this fur-tight mound.
We shall dismantle her; gain Enlightenment.

Master Fontana is the finest anatomist in Florence.
He presses the blade just below the throat, firmly,
enough to slit the hide, leaving intact the membrane –
ignore the yelps and yowls, men. Note the close sleeves
of the Master's robes. Not the fashion, but practical.

Fingers are the most effective tools to lift the skin,
loosening the fascia, working in. A whispering sound,
the separation: if the bitch didn't howl, you'd hear it.

He eases back the blood-matted pelt: the belly throbs.
She is near full term. See the squirming of six pups,
the membranes, here and here, of chorion, allantois,
amnion. It reeks of dog piss: urine often flows.

The Master cuts the pup free: the wet, struggling thing
breathes. It fits in my palm. The mother expires.

Here is a bucket: we shall drown the rest. Unless
you'd like to take one home, gentlemen? One each?
For your little ones to play with?

To 100 parts pure white beeswax, add:

Indigo, 6 parts: for blue shades of eyelid and shadow.
Saffron, 5 parts: for gold-tanned shoulders, hands.
Quercitrin, 9 parts: for olive-yellow skin.
Safflower, 10 parts: for pomegranate lips, and
    Asbestos, powdered: for the shine.
Indigo with Safflower: for the violet of veins.
Dragon's-blood, 6 parts: for the heart's red stain.

## CINTIO

A drowned corpse is often rigid,
victim's face is often livid,
blue be the nails and blue the lips,
jaw and joints are frequently stiff,
froth; water; blood; urine; fluid.
I am haunted by this image,
her skin, my soul – both seem frigid.
Do I question why we do this?
Forgive, forgive.

To once have heard this voice ringing
to think that she was once living!
That someone loved this face, these hips;
I look upon one who is missed:
sighs, perfume, and laughter flinging –
forgive, forgive.

FONTANA

Must I look over my shoulder?
I shall declare the waxwork complete.
This workshop is under my orders –
only perfection will teach.

I shall declare the wax complete
when every corpuscle is red;
only perfection will teach
anatomy of life, not dead.

When every corpuscle is red,
and every pore pressed orange-peel,
anatomy of life, not death,
shall make the minds of Florence kneel.

If every pore, pressed orange-peel,
is gazed at with a hungry eye,
the minds of Florence, as they kneel,
shall never be afraid to die.

When gazing with a hungry eye,
the food is beauty, to the core.
In art, we shall not fear to die
—inspired by a common whore.

Perfect beauty to the core
from patchwork of dismantled souls,
inspired by a common whore,
whose body now we all shall know.

From patchwork of dismantled souls,
Susini works his waxen art.
His creations we shall know,
but I shall choose the Venus Heart.

SUSINI

The glow in candlelight, of Tess. The gift
of fire and green, a shifting tapestry
of flecks and prisms, gold through which she sees.
Wreath of India silk: a perfect fit,
this scarf of regal sheen, in floating drifts.
One wayward, clumsy move – my loving reach
caressing her, from clavicle to knee
but knocking down the candle, so it splits.
It spills across her arm; she jumps, she cries.
I hate that my abstraction brings her pain!
But wait: she calms. She hesitates. She smiles.
My blood begins to swirl. The wicked wiles
in pagan parts step forth. She says, 'Again.'
I bring the candle; on my bed she lies.


TERESA

He brings the candle; on his couch I lie.
He stretches me, lengthwise, across the bed.
Flames of India silk wrap round my head,
obscure my vision; darkness binds my eyes.
Each finger-touch, cool, takes me by surprise,
conjuring *pelle d'oca*. I am sent
into mesmeric states of radiance
as his firm hands and tongue plait my demise.
And then a pause, and then, he drips the wax,
in florets, bronchioles, across my chest.
I know not when – the flash, the hot contact;
my skin, it flinches, dazzled by the act.
Heat. Pain. Pleasure. An orderly distress.
I am reborn, a quail's-egg carapace.

SUSINI

She is reborn. A quail's-egg carapace,
blue gold, as fragile, now encrusts her form.
And in her resurrection, I'm reborn:
a wily god, whom none can put amiss.
Subject to every whim, my young mistress
responds to waxen kiss, her skin as warm.
From any other thoughts, I am foresworn.
In leaning close, I drink her mouth, her lips.
Her matter immaterial. A trick
of light; her coos of worship, small sweet sounds,
enamour me. I smooth, I sculpt; she shifts.
Wax, then flesh, then wax; as soft and sticky;
no more rapturous love could I have found.
The glow in candlelight, of Tess, the gift.

## CINTIO

I am a devilish Cupid.
Is their purity soiled
by the gaze of my ruined face?

They are a flickering instant of grace,
fragile as the frost-fingered lace
crocheting the Arno's banks in winter.

Once, I was pleasant enough.
Once, women smiled at me;
men clasped my hand in greeting.

Riches poured from the Royal Kitchens,
how I was drunk on it all!
Greed was repaid.

I leant over the spit:
fragrant sage, a tender lamb,
sizzling oil in a pan.

A shout from a serving-man.
I spun, protesting – the gall!
My mouth full of flesh.

A crash.
A searing.
A fall. Then, darkness.

My face is numb.
I cannot taste. My tongue,
struck dumb of flavours.

I can speak, but only eat
to live. I earn little.
My life, a constant Lent.

The taste I miss most:
that sage, that lamb.
A ghostly torment.

All the while
I tend rank carcasses,
my stomach turned in disgust.

Is mine a wasted life?
A wasted face, yes.
But I complete my tasks.

I need only an oilcloth cloak and hat,
a pair of boots, my wicker baskets,
some linen rags.

The bead of quicksilver rushed down your waxen form too hastily.
It should have savoured each curve:
the sweep of golden eyebrow,
flick of spun lash,
swoop of delicate nose,
nectar of lips.

*Romantic daydreamer.*
*The drop of mercury rolled*
*down the occipito-frontalis,*
*orbicularis palpebrarum,*
*pyramidalis nasi,*
*orbicularis oris.*

Soft nape of neck,
white curve of throat,
angular clavicle,
snowy décolletage,
swell of breast.

*Sterno-cleo-mastoid,*
*platysma myoides,*
*winged suprasternal notch,*
*between the clavicular notches,*
*pectoralis; mammary.*

The drop rolled over your birthmark
*the congenital melanocytic naevus*

followed your stomach
*down the abdomen*

moved down your thigh
*the vastus externus,*

to the hill of knee
*patella*
alabaster calf
*gastrocnemius muscle*
ballerina ankle
*tendo achillis*
the tips of your toes
*your metatarsals.*

My love, I would have done as much.
*Mio Dio, Susini, concentrate!*

*Act Three*

He lies with her by the Arno.
They smell of honey, of Carthaginian wax
which he strokes with sculptor's fingers.
He dreams, as he works, of her flesh.
His touch leaves smells of pitch, the tint
of linseed oil, while turpentine

scents their love. Turpentine
hides everything. Breezes along the Arno
won't sweep his work away. Green glass: the tint
of her eyes. Lips: dragon's-blood. She's living wax,
and immortal. She loves his hands on her flesh,
how he knows her with his mouth, his fingers.

He spools out whimpers; she runs her fingers
into his hair, shining with sweat, turpentine,
oils from the workshop. She gives her flesh
while birds keen above the Arno
and he drowns in her: rich, not wax,
then wax again. Pliant. The shifting tint

of sunlit water blinds out the tint
of each other's skin. They taste. Twine fingers.
Her legacy will be one of wax,
her suppleness, in pitch and turpentine.
Who will remember her joy by the Arno,
where he traces her honey-scented flesh?

Fontana is haunted by flesh,
heedless of love's tint
on Susini's cheek. The Arno,
a river to cross, while busy fingers
count coins, supplies, turpentine,
worry they won't succeed with the wax.

On hot days, the water flows sluggish, like wax.
In black moods, Fontana gluts on roasted flesh.
Cintio cleans up specimens, turpentine,
fearing Teresa's distraction will taint
Susini's work at La Specola. Fingers
at work should not tarry beside the Arno.

The River Arno whispers to the worker of wax
who uses his fingers on the anatomies, on living flesh.
Pigments, tinted, mingle: liquid honey, transparent turpentine.

TERESA

Morning: heavy rain. Now the clouds
have done with their lament,
and the air, lightened, breathes relief
for their completed confession.

Cloaked against damps and draughts,
I pace the wet darkness of stone walls.
Pluck *lumache* into my pail.

They escape the floods, but not,
I fear, my cooking pot.


FONTANA

Her, Cintio. Her? A woman's? Yes.
Difficult to tell with the hair shorn.

The eyes are narrowed, the nose too short.
But we must assemble a perfect whole
from perfect parts. And her ears
are without flaw.


TERESA

*Lumache:* precious slick creatures
navigating Florentine stones;

your latitudes doom you to my line of sight.
Starving you will feed us in three or four nights.

FONTANA

*Oreccia.* We shall first reveal
the outer ear, then the inner,

the eustachian tubes; delve deep
into the cochlea, semi-circular canals.

Precision, Exactitude, is my muse.
A practised scalpel, a steady hand,

infinite patience. Perfection,
revealed, shall in perfection teach.


TERESA

A handful of grain, my spiralled lovelies.
An offering. Fresh water; a clean pail.
Why do your slick tracks whisper aphrodisiacs?

You slide so gently, your home on your back.
You withdraw, curl up, as we shall withdraw,
curl together, once we have consumed you.

## FONTANA

*Tuba auditiva, canals semicirculares,*
*os petrosum.* Removed from the skull,
this ear (reeking but a little)
is recognizable as an ear
to even the layman. The inside, revealed!

*Tuba auditiva, canals semicirculares.*
(Precision, precision.) *Os petrosum.*


## TERESA

No grain, only water now, *lumache mie.*
Oh, little horns: spiralled, fluted, striped.

Unlikely chunks of flesh. Worth
this slow process. You demand
precision, patience. The harvest,
the cleansing, followed by a purge.

You will go pure into me.

FONTANA

Delicately spiralled and fluted. Stripped
of flesh and excess protection,
I polish these nuanced fragments
which once thrummed, oscillating
into words. Into music?

Tap: I hit petrous temporal bone.
Where is my chisel?


TERESA

Vinegar and salt: it is a coarse business.
Froth and foam. Metamorphoses.

Once animate, your final animation
is this wrenching, writhing dance.

Do not appeal to me: I feasted you
before I ended it. More vinegar.


FONTANA

Smells in the workshop –
turpentine, and a vinegary sourness.
The icteric scent of slowly rotting meat.

But such precision! I will prepare one hundred ears,
see one hundred differences, yet hers represent
an ideal. The perfect ear: tiny spirals.

TERESA

Boil, and then with a fork,
a twist, a pull – revelation.
I clean the flesh. Wipe the slime.
Each springy spiral sits in line.


FONTANA

It is ready. Has it been three days or four?
No matter. A revelation. Before it rots,
Susini will build up wax. Colour. Form
and structure. So life-like as to seem real.

One will wish to speak into it; expect it to listen.
Susini will use his craftsman's fingers,
and I will ensure precision. Accuracy.

We will have spirals, whorls, arches.
I reveal, he creates. The ear
is but a small part.


TERESA

Garlic, butter, olive oil.
Anchovies, fennel, parsley, onion.

Listen: hear how gently they simmer?

White wine, salt, pepper, nutmeg.
Serve very hot off the hearth.

FONTANA

Susini, today we model the *oreccia*.
Note especially the convolutions of the cochlea.


TERESA

Susini, my love, you exhaust yourself,
hunched in that workshop day and night.

I give you a whole, living body in which to delight.
See? Your gift, these silver earrings,
illuminate my neck in the candlelight.

Here: let me feed you.
*Lumache.*

My love, with your scents of sunlight and myrrh: you carry
the greatest gift. Take this crown of oregano, rosemary, bay;

this ring with an emerald like your eyes. We are promised
to one another, and to the planted babe. A humble trinity.

First, he'll be a pine nut; precious woody kernel tucked safe
within your sheaths; evergreen strength yet to be released.

His green pistachio-limbs will begin to take shape, wax-pliant,
and he will branch into humanness slowly, in dark fertile terrain.

His almond-mind will grow sharp; his almond-spirit sweet; dust
of mother's saffron, of father's paints. Patience, stillness, he'll gain.

Head and heart will round with the tenderness of walnut. No
more certain shape: the two sides of brain; left and right hemisphere.

Blessed chestnut will make our child sure. From thence, in range
of mother's womb, his tiny form secure. We with joy await him.

CINTIO

Without the crumb, the wax is incomplete.
A ripened womb, which makes all women less
sublime than angels, and yet more replete.

FONTANA

The Venus, finished, makes the centrepiece.
Susini has eyes only for his Tess:
how will this wax Enlighten when complete?

CINTIO

Contrived in love, she is a masterpiece,
looking like her, whom he admires best.
Sublime, an angel, and yet more replete.

FONTANA

Our Venus is perfection, neutral, sweet:
a waxen heart within a waxen breast.
My power, and the form, is incomplete.


CINTIO

Dare we use *her*? A simple pennyroyal tea.
For through Tess, that crumb may we possess
to make the Venus perfect, and replete.


FONTANA

My Museum moulds around my creed.
Then I shall guide Susini's hand. Impress
the need to use *his* child to complete
the Venus. A deftly-handled feat.

## TERESA

This trinity of herbs becomes me.
This triumph of meat.

Soft holy herbal thyme,
sharp rosemary-sprigged crown,
the pricked, bleeding haunch of lamb.
I prepare this for love of him.

Past our lips the sage.
Onto our tongues the rosemary.
Down our throats the garlic.
Into our bodies the lamb.

Over the hearth, cooking,
I am bound in these herbs.

They will sweat out.

*Tripparoli* cry their goods.
What *carne* do I crave?

*Finole*: marrow of calf's spine.
*Animelle*: pancreas, thymus, brains.
*Granelli*: delicate testicles.

*Cibreo*: cockscombs, wattles, gizzards.
Caterina de'Medici's favoured dish.

*Tripparoli* cry, 'Tripe, trotters and muzzle!'

Crown them all with bay leaves.
Bring them all to me.

*Tripparoli* goods do not appeal to me.
To the shops go I, to buy a soothing tea.
Advice I find: this Apothecary.

SUSINI

My darling lies small in this red sea.
Her pale skin, waxen: I mistake her.
This isn't real.
No warmth. No breath on a glass.

She has left a final,
terrible gift. Part of herself,
a parcel wrapped in silent pain.
I need reason. A reason.

She felt a small discomfort,
drank this tea to ease.
But this hand is cruel familiar –
not an Apothecary's...

One servant brings our stillborns in;
his face reflects a soul of sin.

There's pennyroyal in this tea:
a plan to steal my son from me.

Him I can't forgive.
*Cintio*, *Cintio*.

## CINTIO

I cannot say –
I did not mean –
I mean to say –
The fault is not –
We did not know –
I did not see –
She meant to take –
An accident –
Lies, all lies –
It wasn't meant –
Forgive, forgive –
What seems is not –

## FONTANA

All our hands are bloodied now:
you've strangled my poor Cintio,

I tried to save your wife,
and failed.

There lies the cripple;
there, the babe;

there, your Venus – once alive.
There's one thing left to save.

You must complete the wax, my boy;
alone, you have the skill.

Then, I can protect you,
for my servant, you have killed.

You acted in revenge, it's true,
but law comes after law.

I will appeal to the Grand Duke
to see you are absolved.

You must complete the wax, my son,
and you must use your child.

You made the Venus look like her:
Fate sees it's reconciled.

SUSINI

No greater sorrow have I known
than in this sparrow-weight of bones.
My loves are gone: my bride, my son,
now let me die alone.

A twisted path we all have taken,
now I know I am forsaken.
I took pride in our creation:
I see I was mistaken.

Fontana may be skilled and wise,
but trapped in Cintio's wicked lies,
so if we knew, we turned our eyes
– the Devil's in the compromise.

Without her, I cannot remain,
the blackest bile will rise again;
my spirit will not bear the pain,
and so, to this refrain:

No greater sorrow have I known
than in this sparrow-weight of bones.
Cease you now, sad metronome,
and let me die alone.

*Epilogue*

FONTANA

I will leave my body for dissection.
I understand the need for specimens.

Cintio, our Porter, will be mentioned,
his rounds to the Orphanage and Hospital attended.

Susini and his skill, his melancholy,
his drowning in the Arno: all recorded diligently.

The Duke thinks the waxes the Museum's greatest good,
but I press on – oh, ambition! – carve *anatomies in wood*.


VENUS

Fontana's clumsy wooden models shall never reach
the famous anatomy his waxworks still teach.

His remains will lie in Santa Croce
with Galileo, Michelangelo, Machiavelli.

TERESA / VENUS

I have not turned to stone.
My tallow incandescence
will metamorphose with a skilled touch –
my deaf ears will ripen to sound;
blind eyes dilate to light;
mute lips sigh, at a touch.

I have not turned to stone: malleable yet,
though time has rationed its grains in the glass,
and dust gathers on bloodless skin.

I may only speak what is written for me,
but no, I will not turn to stone.

# ⤳ Notes ⤳

## Drama behind the scenes: enlightenment and passion at the Museo 'La Specola'

Dr Anna Maerker, Historian of Medicine

Author of *Model Experts: Wax Anatomies and Enlightenment in Florence and Vienna, 1775-1815* (Manchester University Press, 2011).

Today's visitors to the Museo 'La Specola' in Florence discover an oasis of calm among the bustle of biology students and researchers from the local university. Behind rooms filled with stuffed animals and impaled insects the museum holds a unique collection of wax models of the human body: life-sized, beautiful men and women, serenely reclining on silk cushions behind glass. 'Lo Spellato', the flayed man, seems remarkably calm for one who has lost his skin.

However, behind the quiet exterior of the anatomical collection today there are the stories of the men and women who made them. The Tuscan Grand Duke Pietro Leopoldo, a younger son of Austrian Empress Maria Teresa, arrived in Tuscany aged eighteen, his head filled with the latest ideas of the enlightened *philosophes*, determined to turn his new territory into a model state. Together with his court scientist, Felice Fontana, he devised a new kind of place: a public museum, open to all free of charge. Pietro Leopoldo and Fontana took the remains of the old Medici cabinet of curiosities, went on a shopping trip to the scientific capitals of Paris and London, and created a collection designed to display nature in all its forms – from minerals and plants to animals and machines. Last but certainly not least, the museum was to display the most intricate machine of all – man himself. To encourage visitors to engage with the collection, everything was to be beautiful. No shrivelled body bits floating in jars, then, but shapely wax bodies in lively poses and colours. The presentation of the models, accompanied by schematic drawings, was intended to impress upon the visitor a total view of the human body, and provide an immediate understanding of the underlying natural laws. In director Fontana's words, 'at one glance everything is seen, everything is known'. In practice, however, this process was far from simple. Tensions and conflicts were hidden behind the models' serene exterior.

Models were produced at a workshop in the museum itself. The Grand Duke bestowed upon his new institution the privilege to use unclaimed bodies from the local hospital and the orphanage. The museum's factotum, the unfortunate Giacinto Guidetti, made his rounds daily, carrying body parts across town in his wicker basket. Once delivered to the museum, the bodies were turned into preparations by anatomists like Tommaso Bonicoli. The preparations, then, served as templates for the artists who sculpted the wax models – as models for the models. This process was not without its problems. The Grand Duke and his court scientist were fortunate in the crucial availability of modelling know-how: for centuries, Florentine artists and artisans had used materials such as wax to produce votive offerings in the shape of body parts, and portrait busts depicting local saints and dignitaries. The now defunct Medici dynasty had patronized the celebrated artist and clergyman Gaetano Zumbo, who used wax to create miniaturized scenes of death and decay which served as *memento mori*, reminders of mortality. Thus, when the museum was founded, the Grand Duke and Fontana could draw on considerable skills and traditions embodied in sculptors like Giuseppe Ferrini and Clemente Susini.

The collaboration was fraught with tensions. The passionate Grand Duke impatiently awaited the creation of a model collection to create model citizens – preferably on time, and on budget. The irascible director Felice Fontana considered himself the ultimate arbiter of anatomical truth, and the artists mere 'tools' in his hands. The artists, however, had their own claims to anatomical expertise. Their skills were rare and frequently admired by visitors. Thus encouraged, they resisted Fontana's attempts to discipline them – administrative records and increasingly exasperated letters of complaint by Fontana describe how the artists were late for work, how they drank hot chocolate, swore, and played practical jokes on the apoplectic director.

Archival records also reveal other invisible contributors to La Specola's exceptional project of public enlightenment, from the parish priests who encouraged their congregations to donate marvels of nature to the museum, to the Florentine husband who brought his wife's stillborn, and the seamstresses who delicately stitched fragile dried plants to display boards. With a keen eye for detail, artists Kelley Swain and Tanya Marcuse bring the models and their humans to life again today.

## Phantom Bodies

Tanya Marcuse, Photographer

www.tanyamarcuse.com/wax-bodies

In the summer of 2006, I began photographing wax anatomical models in a small museum in Florence known as 'La Specola', The Royal Museum of Physics and Natural History – born at the height of the Enlightenment. The museum is on the third floor of a building that is now part of the University of Florence, just ᐧ down the street from the Pitti Palace, on the Via Romana.

A maze-like series of rooms display birds' nests, starfish, ostrich eggs, and stuffed mammals. Foxes and sharks have large, visible stitches, making the process of preservation keenly physical. At the end of this maze of taxidermy is a surprising group of rooms. These rooms house over fourteen hundred wax anatomical models and drawings. Grids of glass cases line all four walls of each room containing models of fragments of the body – hearts, eyes, brains, and limbs. Models of whole bodies punctuate each room. Flayed male figures stand in upright glass cases. Women recline in Snow White-like cases; they lie on satin sheets and silken cushions, complete with cascading hair, pearl necklaces, and lovingly sculpted fingers and toes. Their bodies are opened, revealing their internal organs, their heads thrust back, lips parted, eyes toward heaven – in rapture.

The so-called 'Phantom Bodies' were created to reveal new knowledge of the body, anatomy, childbirth and disease. In the 18th century 'La Specola' functioned both as a workshop to make the models as well as a museum open to popular public viewings. The process of making the models was a meticulous intersection of art and science, with a sculptor working alongside an anatomist. Models were based on anatomical illustrations highlighting recent discoveries. A man named Giacinto Guidetti made documented rounds at the two hospitals in Florence to collect cadavers and fragments of cadavers – adults from Santa Maria Nuova and children and babies from the hospital of the orphanage Instituto degl'Innocenti. The dissector arranged the bodies to match the illustration, sometimes using numerous cadavers to create an illusion of a whole body. Plaster moulds were taken directly from the body parts, as well as modeled indirectly, through observation. Pigmented molten wax was poured into the moulds in thin layers. To make lifelike membranes and vessels, thin metal and textile threads were covered in wax. The finished model was varnished to create the believable look of moist flesh. It could take as long as six months to create a model of a 'whole' body.

Besides 'La Specola,' I also photographed the collection of models at the Josephinum in Vienna (once the Military Surgical-Medical Academy in the 1780s). These Viennese models were made in Florence at 'La Specola.' The Emperor Joseph II saw the Florentine models ready for display on a visit to his brother, the Grand Duke of Tuscany, and ordered a duplicate set for Vienna with the hopes that these 'phantom bodies' would provide a breakthrough in the teaching of medicine with a shortage of real cadavers for students to work with. The models and their transport (1,192 wax models travelled on the backs of mules across the Alps from Florence to Vienna between 1784 and 1786) were extremely costly, but he felt sure they would bring down the mortality rate at the Military Surgical-Medical Academy. In fact, for these purposes, the models were a complete and well-documented failure. The two collections are, in theory, identical. Yet their differences are intriguing – the Italian women have olive complexions and lush brown hair, while the Viennese are pale, blue-eyed and blond, and wear golden circlets.

In the beginning, I had set out to treat the models in a typological way, centred and restrained, cool, and categorical – in black and white. I had never photographed in colour. This approach seemed in keeping with the Enlightenment roots of the models themselves. But what I 'saw' instead often seemed closer to a dream. In fact, for the years I worked on this project I dreamed often of the models' vivid faces, and opened bodies. I found myself haunted by the mystery of the identities of the men, women and babies that were used to make the models.

Many of the ornate cases still have the original 18th-century glass – wavy and filled with tiny bubbles. In the beginning of the project I used black cloths to reduce or eliminate reflections, trying to get a clear picture of the models inside. But as the project evolved, the reflections – whether sublime, obscuring or transforming – became central to the series. I began to allow the reflections on the surface of the glass to merge with the wax figure inside the case (Nº 120), or in some photographs the reflection becomes a dress lending modestly to a figure stripped bare of all skin, except her pubic area (Nº 11 and Nº 116). Streaked with dust and reflecting rows of fluorescent lights, the glass often obscures and transforms, rather than reveals, the wax models. In Wax Bodies I came to see the medium of photography as an analogue to Enlightenment concepts of seeing and understanding the world. Both have the look of truth, with a stranger fiction not far beneath the surface.